She Died And You Killed Her

Poems of Grief

April Worth

BookLeaf
Publishing

India | USA | UK

Made with ❤ on the BookLeaf Publishing Platform
www.bookleafpub.in
www.bookleafpub.com

Dedication

For My Angel Friend

Who left this world too soon
But never left my heart
Every word in these pages carries your light
I write because you lived freely
I healed because you loved warmly

Forever paddling beside me

Preface

Dear Reader,

I didn't write this book to be known. I wrote it because I had to. Because for years, I carried the weight of ghosts— of grief, of trauma, of the versions of myself that were destroyed along the way. I have died a thousand deaths, some at the hands of others, some by my own. This book is their burial and their resurrection.

She Died and You Killed Her is a collection of poems mapping my healing journey—from the storm to the wreckage, through the haunting, and into my rebirth. It is for the girl who drowned in sorrow and the woman who learned to breathe again. It is for anyone who has ever been shattered and is still searching for their way back to themselves.

To those who have felt lost in life: may these words remind you that even in the darkest depths, you are never beyond saving.

Love,
April

Acknowledgements

To my mom—thank you for never giving up on me, for loving me deeply through it all, and for choosing to heal alongside me. Your unwavering support has been a light in my darkest moments.

To my dad—thank you for learning to meet me where I am, for grounding me, and for taking me on a life-changing trip to Antarctica, where I could finally see just how much I've grown. That journey reshaped me in ways I will never forget.

To my vocal coach and sister in Christ, Rose—your guidance and encouragement have given my voice strength, not just in music but in life.

To my loyal companion, Parsnip—your unconditional love and emotional support have helped me reach new heights of confidence. You are a true therapy dog.

To my wellness team—thank you for your passion, love, and kindness in restoring my health. Dr. Rez, Dr. Whit, Dr. Joni, Dr. Charlotte, Master Choa Kok Sui, Lama Lobsang Palden, Julie S., Julie K.,Tom, Sabrina, Niykee, Healing Arts Center, Willow Place, and my therapy horse Pistol will always hold a special place in my heart.

To my family, friends, and clients—your belief in me, especially as I built my massage therapy career and opened my own practice, Lighthouse Touch, has been nothing short of a dream realized. I am endlessly grateful.

And to God—for blessing me with the divine gift to work His magic through my hands. Every healing touch, every word on these pages, is a testament to His grace.

1. Trust In Time

A walking tower moment
A curve ball
A conscious exit
A holy liar
A conduit broken
A focus, held proof
A gun for hire
A twisted fate
A truth untold
A silent screen
A heart gone cold
A path unchosen
A bridge on fire
A soul undone
A thread, now fray, and tangled in the wire
A moment priced
A moment forgiven
A heart once shattered
A soul, still driven
A truth concealed

A love, once given
A road less traveled
A light, still hidden
A tear unspoken
A hope, yet driven
A life reformed
A new path written
A place reclaimed
A spirit risen
A fleeting time
But forever, we're living

2. Eyes

Why climb to reach a high I've already received?
Where did you place your eyes?
23 kisses planted right onto my left cheek
Fabricated lies
Drove by my cold streak of losing
I was dating a fiend
Well your stare makes my eyes drip
Slow
To the floor
Pretend play roughly with me
For sure
Discreetly disguise my mind
Certainly disarm
Keep still
Where, oh where, where did you place your eyes?
Where, oh where, where did you place your eyes?
Damn I tap out
Making me show off
Call it
Lash out

Get high to cool off
Cut the soul tie
The common lie
That I would be the one to fix you
Where did you place your eyes?
Whimsical
Dodgy
The softest pull
Shove me
Forever I'll recognize calculated eyes
Well your stare makes my heart hurt
Falsely cured
Challenged by your feedback
That's rich
Too firm
Secretly steal my time
Where, oh where, where did you place your eyes?
Where, oh where, where did you place your eyes?
Damn I tap out
Making me show off
Call it
Lash out
Get high to cool off
Cut the soul tie
The common lie
That I would be the one to fix you
Where did you place your eyes?

Morning Glory, what's your story?
I got high and now I'm boring
Morning Glory, what's your story?
I got burned and now I'm boring
Morning Glory, what's your story?
Where did you place your eyes?

3. You Existed

Have you ever held a memory so tightly
that it left imprints on your palms,
like the faintest echo of something real,
something slipping, something gone?

Did you press it to your chest at night,
afraid the dawn would steal its shape?
Did you whisper to it like a prayer,
begging time to let it stay?

Did it change beneath your fingertips,
softened edges, colors blurred?
Did it quiet into something distant,
a song half-sung, a voice unheard?

And when it finally slipped away,
unraveled thread, a fading light,
did you wonder if it ever happened
or only lived inside your mind?

4. To Stomach You

I tried to hold you
Tried to make room
For the weight of your chaos
But my body knew better
Each word you spoke
A stone too sharp swallow
Each betrayal
Acid rising in my chest
I bent myself
Into every shape
To accommodate your storm
But it spilled over
Poisoning the well of me.
My body revolted
Ten days purging
What my soul
Could no longer bear
Violent tremors
A rejection of everything
You poured into me

It wasn't weakness
It was survival
My stomach became my guide
Turning inside out
To rid me of the toxins
I once called friendship
That freedom never looked like
The weight that followed
The quiet gnawing
Of memories I couldn't place
The echo of promises
Made by the hands that never cared
About my worth
I became a map
Of places I shouldn't have gone
Now I've learned
Some people aren't meant to stay
Some bonds aren't worth
The cost of your own peace
To stomach you
Was to lose myself
And I won't be lost again.

5. Misused

I carry light in my hands
Offered it freely
A lantern for the lost
A warmth for the cold
But my glow was never enough

It became a mirror
Reflecting their shadows
And when they saw themselves
They called me the flame
That burned them

My kindness was currency
Spent by hands that never asked
If I had enough to give
They took until I was hollow
Then cursed the echo that remained

When the darkness found me
And I clutched my last ember

Close to my chest
They called me selfish
A villain cloaked in my own pain

But they never saw
The years of quiet sacrifice
How i turned my own heart
Into a harbor
For their storms

But I've learned
My light was never meant
To blind or burn
Only to guide me
Back to myself

6. If Gravity Was Food

If gravity was food
I'd already be full
No need for seconds
No plate to hold the weight
I've carried in silence
The toll has been paid
In moments too heavy
To speak aloud
In footsteps that sunk deep
Into the earth
If gravity was food
It would taste of iron and salt
A bittersweet feast
That clings to the tongue,
That nourishes and depletes
In equal measure.
No table could bear
What I've been served
No recipe could soften
The pull of its grip

But if gravity was food,
I'd learn to savor the weight
To let it ground me,
Feed the roots
That hold me steady,
So I can rise
Full
And free

7. Had To

It's always your side
I fell through
Distorted comebacks
If only you knew
Undertaken
Wide-eyed
Mistaken
Gaslight
No Score
The obsession took form
Big enough
Enforced
Unwarned
Tricked by fables
Read coarse
Inhaled noxious discourse
And I...
Shelf life on credit
No proof
No edit

And I had to let go, had to let go, had to let go
Whole-hearted
Pulled back
And I saw it
Departed
Got bitchy
To solve it
Thank God
I indirectly heal the past
As I honor the price of peace
The obsession took form
Big enough
Enforced Unwarned
Tricked by fables
Read coarse
Inhaled noxious
Discourse
And I...
Shelf life on credit
No proof
No edit
And I had to let go, had to let go, had to let go
Of when
I shared my body with you
I'm damn near impatient
For healing the joke
Of exchanging numbers with you

Oh my soul was present
When I bared my body to you

15

8. 2013 - 2017

Echoes fill the void,
Years collapse beneath the weight
A silence that screams

Your absence, a wound
Days blurred in a heavy haze
I still felt your love

Time stopped in your name
Grief became my only truth
I learned how to breathe

Whisper at her grave
"I am not here, I've moved on"
Grace blooms in the wind

9. Short-lived

I think you loved me like the wind
Fleeting brilliance in the way you grew
Bending to your touch, yet free to roam
A whispered warmth, then gone too soon

Free fall
My worth
Free fall
Back to Earth

I think you held me like the tide
Pulling close, then slipping through
Soft embrace that felt like home
Yet never meant to follow through

Drifting
My fate
Drifting
It's too late

I think you knew me like the dawn
Brief and bright, a passing grace
A tender glow that kissed my soul
Then faded, leaving empty space

Burning
My heart
Burning
From the start

10. Forgive Me

I'm not sure when the quiet settled
when the spaces between us grew
if it was a slow unraveling
or a thread pulled too soon

I search my heart for missing pieces
for words I should have said
but time has turned them into echoes
soft as footprints that once were tread

I wish I could have told you then
I was shedding skin, coming undone
trapped inside a storm of silence
too weak to reach for anyone

My body ached, my mind was heavy
I was drowning, lost and low
I had to let a part of me die
the one that couldn't heal or grow

I hope you understand someday
that my distance wasn't you
but a battle fought in quiet rooms
a life rebuilt from something new

But if you ever pause and wonder
if my name still lingers near
know that I have only kindness
only wishes meant sincere

I hope you're well, I hope you're happy
I hope life is kind to you
and if ever our paths cross again
I hope the light still feels true

11. I'm Sorry

A little unnerving
It's your call
Hold it or fall back
Noticed
Noted
You were my dog
The only one I called on at night
You were stupid tall and sexy
It could have been a dream
It was a dream
When I was young and lonely
Profoundly depressed and I just became
Obsessed with you
And I'm sorry
I'm sorry I broke you
I'm sorry I cared
I'm sorry I came through
I'm sorry I disappeared
I've grown up now
I can only sing

For the ones that need it
Because I have faith in all my words
And I can only pray that you feel it
When you were young and lonely
Black and blue
Not immune to my frantic magery
And I'm sorry
I'm sorry I broke you
I'm sorry I cared
I'm sorry I came through
I'm sorry I disappeared
Not sure when I fell out of love
But like a bruise
I heal

12. Mountain Cure

Each time my soul cracks open
The mountains call me
Whispers on the wind
That only my heart can hear
First, Asheville
Where mist kissed the earth
And the trees held secrets
In their ancient roots
There, I felt the earth pulse beneath my feet
Each vibration unlocking doors inside me
Releasing the emotions I thought I'd buried
Then Colorado Springs
Where the air was thin
But my spirit soared
As if the peaked reached into my chest
And pulled out the pain I had forgotten
The mountains there didn't ask
They simply took
And now Ushuaia
At the world's end

Where the mountains done just rise
They command
And vibrate through my bones
Shake the fragments of old wounds loose
Until I stand whole
Reset
Reborn
The mountains have a way of pulling
Pulling you to place
Pulling things out of you
You didn't know you could live without
But when they release you
You are lighter
You are free
And you are ready
To begin again

13. 10,000 Angels

I closed my eyes
And the weight of the world
Began to fall

A light, not harsh but hold
Bloomed behind my eyelids
And there they were
10,000 faces

Each one aglow
With a love I could not measure
They spoke in unison
Not with words
But with a resonance
That wrapped around my heart
You are safe
You are loved
We see you, and we are proud

Their gaze stitched the fractures

I had hidden from the world
Their hands cradled
The broken pieces of my soul
As if each shard
Were a treasure
And as I stood there
In the presence of wings and warmth
They whispered a promise
The dreams you thought
Too far, too fragile
They are yours
They are already unfolding

When the vision faded
I wasn't lighter
I was fuller
Filled with their light
Their love
Their certainty

10,000 angels
And for the first time
I believed them

14. Way Down

I've been greatly called upon
Swallowed by the ocean
A cheeky savant kisses during
Applied my notes
It's a given we're thirsty
Unavoidable lurking
One of the nicest guys
Ah hell
I'll just duct tape it back together
Because Honey, you're a mood
And I've been through it
Another word for clever
Quickly burnt out
Been a couple months now
Quickly turns out
I get everything I want, yeah
Quickly turn around
They're all waiting for a show now
Way Down
Way Down

Way Down
Swallowed by the ocean
One of the nicer scars

15. Heart Talk

I wrote you a letter
And I burned it
Then a black feather flew into my face
I move at a graceful pace

Steady eyes comfort exhaustion
I stand taller than your fortune
Topic changed
Gloss the conversation
I'm done
So loved

Heard you out
And I forgot it
Befriended my brain
And I don't regret it

A gold leaf fell
Right on my lip
Heart Talk

Road Map

Infused bright with new intention
I bathe in moonlight for raw reflection
I took it hard
Now I'm quick on my feet
Come clean
See me

16. Portal Point

At Portal Point, I buried myself in snow
Beneath the weight of winds
That howled like ancient spirits
A harsh symphony that kept me awake
The icy rain biting at my skin
The cold creeping into my bones
I felt the nausea rise
But it wasn't just the sickness
It was the weight of the place
The pressure to prove I was strong
To myself, to the earth beneath me
To the stars watching through the dark
Spirit called me here
To face the cold
To stand in the storm
And know my own power
And though I trembled
There was a silent peace within
A deep knowing
That I could withstand it all

He was there
His presence a warmth
Against the relentless chill
His voice cutting through the wind
"Good morning, honey"
And I knew
This moment, this place
Had stitched something between us
That time couldn't erase
I dreamt of humpback whales
Their vastness a reflection of my own
And listened to icebergs capsize
Their cracks like the sound of breaking limits
In this fever dream
I realized
I am a warrior for doing this
And maybe, just maybe
He is my future
Wrapped in the strength of a shared journey
Our hearts echoing against the Antarctic silence

17. Growing Forward

Freshly, I took off, heart alight
A path unknown, a quiet fight
The world ahead, a dream to claim
Yet doubts still whisper, play their game

I dumped old fears, left them behind
Outnumbered by the hopes I'd find
Focus sharp, a vision keen
The future bright, a peaceful sheen

With shrouded faith, I step anew
A journey forged by strength I grew
Each moment, pleasant, yet unknown
And in this route, I stand alone

But in this space, I've grown so much
A deeper love, a braver touch
Though the road ahead may twist and bend
My heart will guide me to the end

18. Boundless

New lands call our names
Hearts unburdened, wild and free
Love keeps leading us

Mountain air so crisp
We climb higher, side by side
Breathless but alive

Jungle hums at dusk
Golden light on tangled paths
We walk hand in hand

Passport ink still fresh
Yet his touch is what I chase
Love, the grandest trip

19. Wishes Granted

In dreams, I traveled lands untold
Where mountains rise and oceans fold
A wanderer, a heart set free
I followed whispers meant for me

Gridworker magic in my hands
Touching earth, creating strands
Of fate that twined and wove me here
To this place where love is clear

A union under skies so vast
The Madonna Inn, a love so fast
Mirroring the love I found
Across the world, where hearts are bound

I thank my younger self each day
For courage, strength, for leading the way
Through trials, tears, and fears untold
To arrive at love, both pure and bold

Now here I stand, with open eyes
Underneath the vast, starlit skies
Grateful for the journey made
For every step, for every trade

This love, this life, this dream fulfilled
A story written, now instilled,
In every breath, in every kiss
A promise kept, a perfect bliss

20. Angelic Flow

Words flow from my soul
Angels guard and guide the path
God speaks through my pen

Silent, I surrender
Divine whispers fill the page
Heaven's touch is near

Pen in hand, I write
Protections placed in every word
Angels stand beside

Through my hand, they speak
Divine light within each line
Guided, I am whole

Automatic flow
God's truth in every letter
Angels watch over

With each word, I hear
Angels' wings and sacred light
God's will through my hands

21. Impact

It was the Sun
Then it was the moonlight
It was the time to trust there's a way
I'm saving my tips in a sparkly blue box
For the Carnival in Venice
I'll go to someday
Odd jobs storytelling
Come over I'll be waiting
Take a chance
Roll the dice
This is my very best life
From the dark to the light
Feel the truth and make it right
Happiness I will find
Before I know I'm in my prime
Smoke signals in the stars
Heat up the night like a spark
Gaining momentum of beyond
Only make my self-love strong
My emotion cascades

I'm ready to hit the waves
A feeling no one can replace
The impact of a solid chase
It was the deer
In the woods
With her babies
Stomping her feet
Huffing at me
It was the storm
And the fog
Giving it's warning
Come closer you'll see
Everything bleeds
It was the trees
In the breeze
I could feel it
A chance to succeed
Right there with me
Circle back a moment
Rewire the loss to presence
Take a chance
Roll the dice
This is my very best life
From the dark to the light
Feel the truth and make it right
Happiness I will find
Before I know I'm in my prime

Smoke signals in the stars
Heat up the night like a spark
Gaining momentum of beyond
Only make my self-love strong
My emotion cascades
I'm ready to hit the waves
A feeling no one can replace
The impact of a solid chase

www.ingramcontent.com/pod-product-compliance
Lightning Source LLC
La Vergne TN
LVHW021304200726
843509LV00012B/1776